REVENGE OF THE TROUT ZOMBIES

A Rollicking River of Trout Fishing Humor

Bruce Cochran

 WILLOW CREEK PRESS

This book is dedicated to the Heart Of America Fly Fishers,
who inadvertently provided at least half the material for it.

Published by Willow Creek Press
P.O. Box 147, Minocqua, Wisconsin 54548
www.willowcreekpress.com

All day you drift through some of the most beautiful scenery in the world, yet you see it not.

The majestic bluffs, the bald eagle soaring on thermals high above you, the snow-capped mountains in the distance, all go unnoticed…

...because your world consists only of that tiny plastic sphere or wisp of colorful yarn... your strike indicator.

You stare at it, hypnotized, as it floats in the current, carrying with it all your hopes, your dreams, and yes... your humanity. You have ceased to function as a living person. An almost imperceptible twitch of your indicator, signaling a strike, is all that can rescue you from the ranks of the living dead. Yes, you have become...

...a TROUT ZOMBIE!

You will drift in your sub-human stupor until you can summon the will to occasionally wrench your eyes from that tyrannical indicator and see the fawn sipping from the water's edge or the osprey soaring above you.

THE COMPLETE TROUT FISHERMAN

NOT SHOWN
Polypropylene underwear that wicks perspiration away from your body and directly to other people's noses

Double visor hat with mesh side panels and chin strap. Available in periwinkle, coral, sage, or moonberry

Impact resistant polarized sun glasses with polycarbonate lenses

Forceps for disengaging hook from trout's mouth (or pinching yourself to see if you're dreaming)

100% wool fingerless gloves

Clippers for snipping monofilament (or performing streamside vasectomies)

Hand made fast action nine foot krypton/boron fly rod with Portuguese cork grip

Stomach pump to determine what trout are feeding on (can be used on self in case of bad pizza)

Blood knot that took four hours to tie

Landing net with teak wood frame (never used since all trout are released)

Yarn strike indicator made from belly fur of virgin mountain sheep (Formerly known as a bobber)

Large arbor machined aluminum/titanium reel filled with neutral density double-tapered fly line

Dry fly floatant (can be used as lip balm in case of emergency)

Aluminum fold-up wading staff with imported cork handle

Invisible size 28 baetis emerger with antron nymphal shuck

Genuine PVC leather wading boots with padded cuffs and felt soles cut from surface of Las Vegas crap table

Breathable poly/cotton vest with 750 pockets. Large rear pocket contains $300 rain jacket and lunch of tofu, brie, and Perrier.

$480 miracle fabric, breathable puncture resistant, stocking foot chest waders with built-in gravel guards and reinforced knee pads

PEOPLE you'll meet ON THE STREAM

ORVILLE OLDGUY

Fishes with a bamboo rod and uses a World War One knapsack for a creel. Dishes out torrents of unsolicited advice and tells you all about how it was back in '32. Always seems to catch fish, but ask him what he's using and he'll tell you, "Fifty years of experience, Sonny."

SAMMY SECRET

Sammy is a retired CIA or FBI agent. He's catching trout on every cast and guarding his fly so no one can see it. If you ask what he's using he'll mumble something unintelligible and turn his back on you.

CEDRIC CELLPHONE

When he's not receiving a call he's making one. In a loud voice he shares his conversations with you and everyone else on the stream. None of the calls are important. He just wants everyone to think he's a very busy person.

PERCY PERFECT

Percy looks like he just stepped out of the pages of a high-dollar angling catalog. He has all the latest clothing and equipment and it always looks brand new. He knows the Latin names of every aquatic insect and will correct you if you call an *Ephemerella Subvari* a Hendrickson.

ILLITERATE IGOR

Igor plops his lawn chair and bait bucket down right between the FLIES ONLY and CATCH AND RELEASE signs, then commences to crank in trout and put them on a big rusty metal stringer. When he's ticketed he claims he didn't know the rules.

RUPERT RUDE

He wades right through the water you're fishing and casts over your line. When his line becomes tangled with yours, he solves the problem by snipping your fly off.

LONNIE LOCAL

Lonnie is seventeen years old, lives five minutes from the stream, and fishes it every afternoon after school. He's wearing cut-off jeans and doesn't need a vest because he only uses two flies, which he carries in a snuff can. Yet he's catching three times as many fish as you with your expensive equipment.

CHATTY CHUCKY

You went fishing to enjoy some solitude but Chucky doesn't care. He'll tell you and everyone else around him his life story, whether you want to hear it or not. He'd show you his operation scar if he could pull his waders down far enough.

LARRY LOUD

Larry is Chucky's first cousin. He yells at his buddies several hundred yards away, whoops and hollers every time he hooks a fish, and swears loudly when he loses one or misses a strike.

As trout streams become more crowded, tempers flare and nasty confrontations occur, often resulting in unfortunate incidents of...

RIVER RAGE!

The following stories are true, told by ordinary anglers victimized by RIVER RAGE...

When an uncouth spin fisherman ridiculed my salmon colored fishing shirt, referring to it as *pink*, I felt my manhood threatened and struck him with my bamboo fly rod. Being only a two weight, however, it did little damage. The cad then ripped my forceps from my vest and twisted my ear lobe with them, causing me to howl in pain.

While rowing my client to a well-known honey hole
I was cut off by another guide. When I complained,
he beat my client with an oar, knocking him out
of the boat and costing me a healthy tip.

I was enjoying a fine summer afternoon of angling on a popular river when I was interrupted by a group of teenaged hooligans in a rubber boat who floated right over my elk hair caddis. When I objected, I was subjected to rude hand gestures and was told to perform an impossible act with my fly rod.

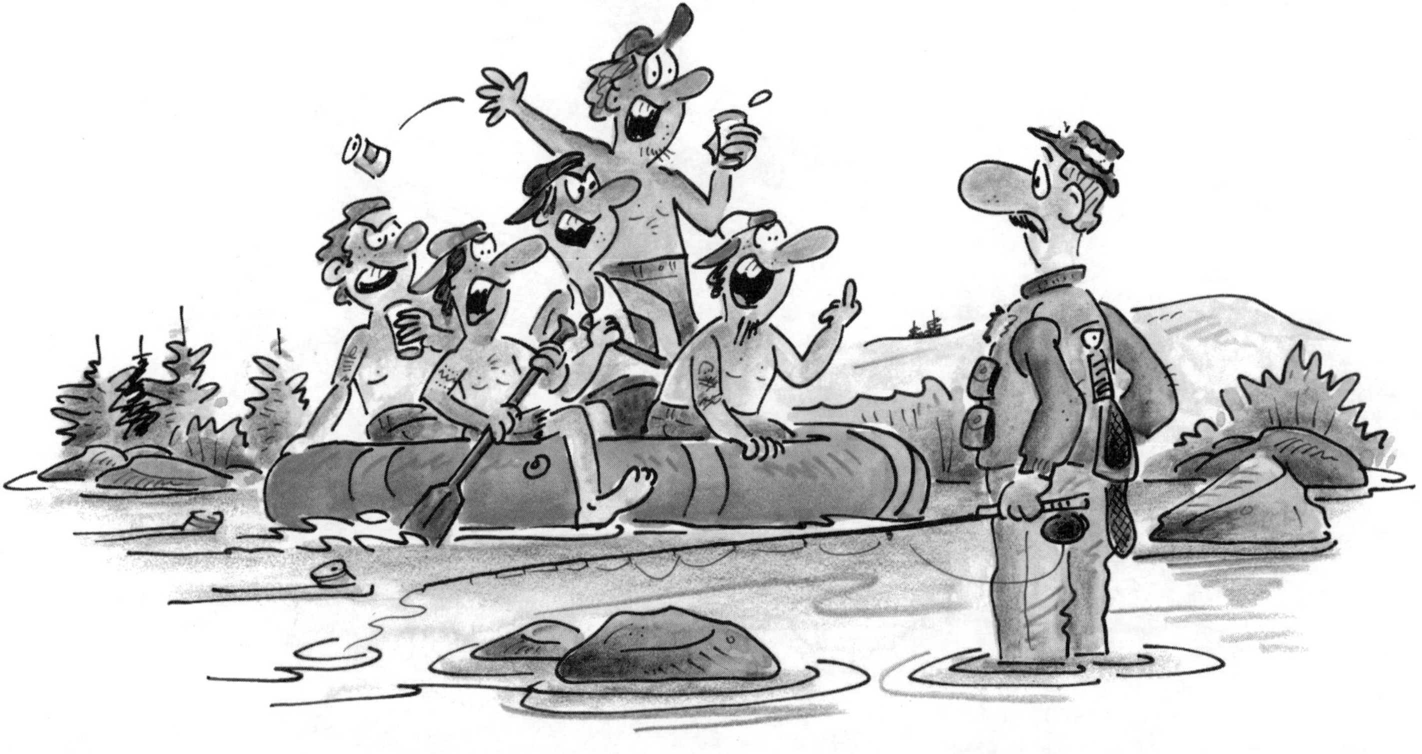

While wading a well-known stream I came upon a group of rough-looking men obviously using night crawlers in a FLIES ONLY area. When I threatened to report them, they pummeled me with their fists and smashed my Winston three weight.

While fishing a public area, I came upon an old man seated in a lawn chair, fishing with bait. Being a fly fisherman, I assumed I had the right of way and waded through the water directly in front of him, nearly hooking him with my back cast. He leapt to his feet, made a rude comment about "damn fly fishermen," and hurled a jar of salmon eggs at me, striking me in the head and knocking my $75 hat into the water.

THE TROUT FISHING
Hall OF *Fame*

In 1951, while attempting to tie a #22 midge emerger onto a 7X tippet, **KRIS "KICKBOAT" KILROY** invented twenty-six new swear words, none of which can be repeated here.

While having his picture taken in 1947, **DINO "DOUBLEHAUL" DUGAN** was the first angler to discover that, by holding a medium-size trout toward the camera at arm's length, he could make it appear much larger.

In 1935
BART "BEADHEAD" BAKER
discovered dry fly floatant while tying on a parachute
Adams after medicating himself with hemorrhoid
ointment and failing to wash his hands.

Tackle dealers will be forever indebted to
WALTER "WOOLLYWORM" WATKINS
who in 1971 discovered that, by painting a common
bobber a solid fluorescent color instead of red and white,
anglers would pay twice as much for it.

In 1947
GUILLERMO "GLOWBALL" GALLAMORE
caught a very large brown trout which he intended to fillet and eat, but while attempting to stuff it into his creel, the fish escaped. Ashamed of his ineptitude, Glowball acted like he had released the fish on purpose, gaining the admiration of his fellow anglers and initiating what we know today as "catch and release."

On a windy day in 1982, high school student
BOBBY "BLOOD KNOT" BLEDSOE
started the piercing fad when he hooked himself in the nose with a
#10 woollybugger. Unable to dislodge the fly, he wore it to school
the next day, where his fellow students thought it was cool.

In 1976, when a blue winged olive hatch mysteriously occurred inside his waders, **ROLLIE "ROLL CAST" ROBERTSON** developed the practice of shuffling to disturb the stream bottom and attract trout.

Jake and Slim had been in the back country for weeks—camping, hiking, and fishing remote lakes and clear mountain streams. Finally their loneliness became unbearable and they sought solace and comfort in one another on...

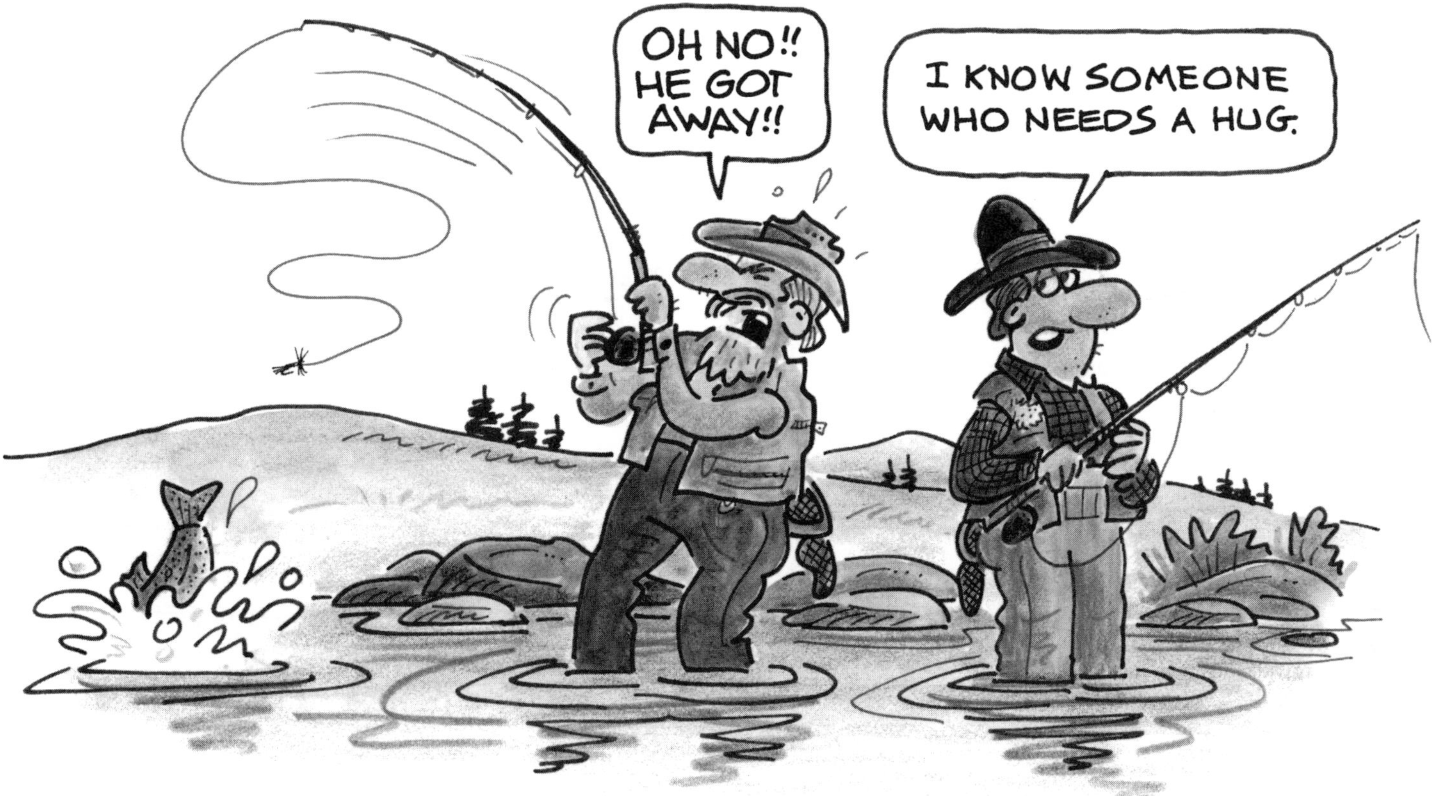
OH NO!! HE GOT AWAY!!
I KNOW SOMEONE WHO NEEDS A HUG.

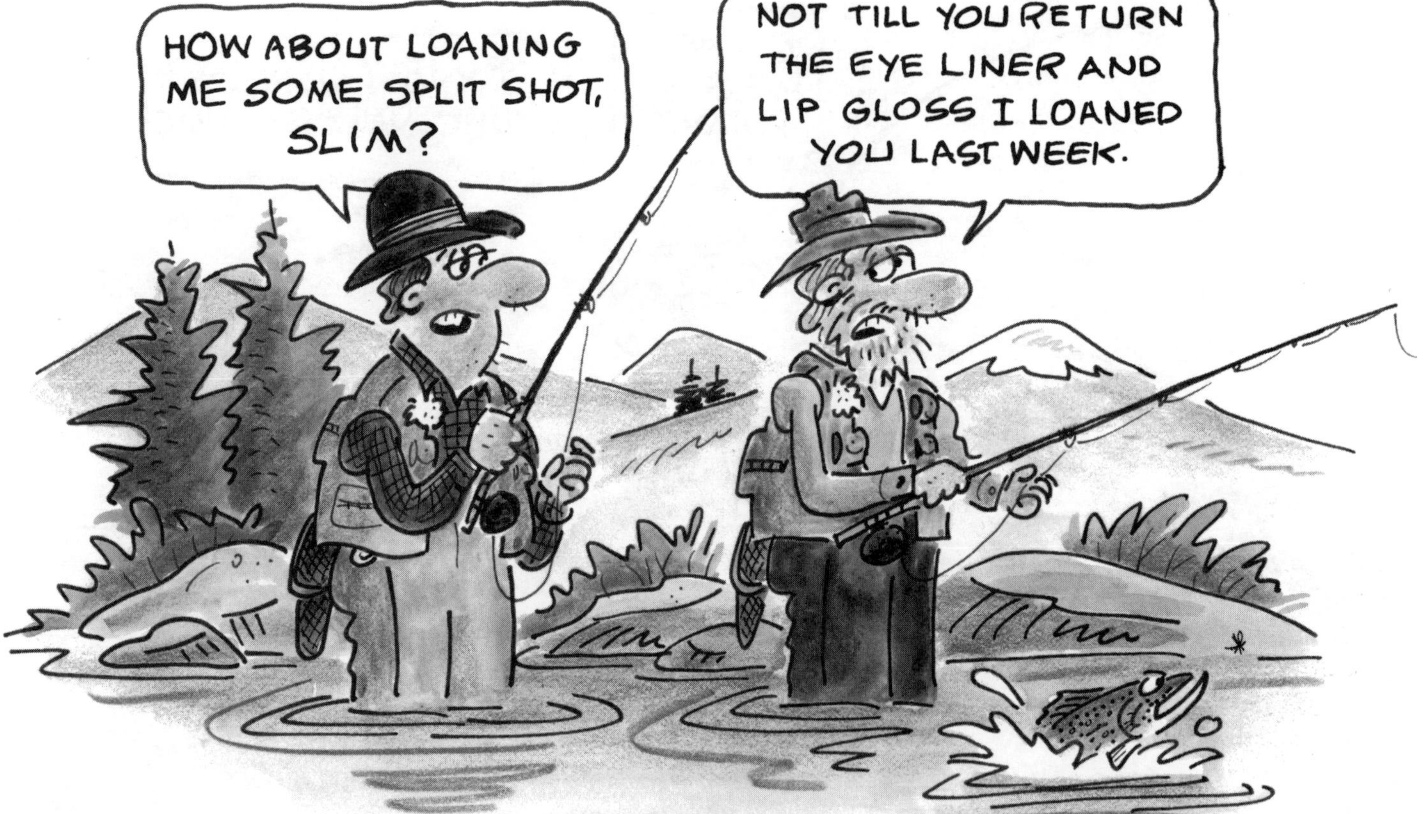
HOW ABOUT LOANING ME SOME SPLIT SHOT, SLIM?
NOT TILL YOU RETURN THE EYE LINER AND LIP GLOSS I LOANED YOU LAST WEEK.

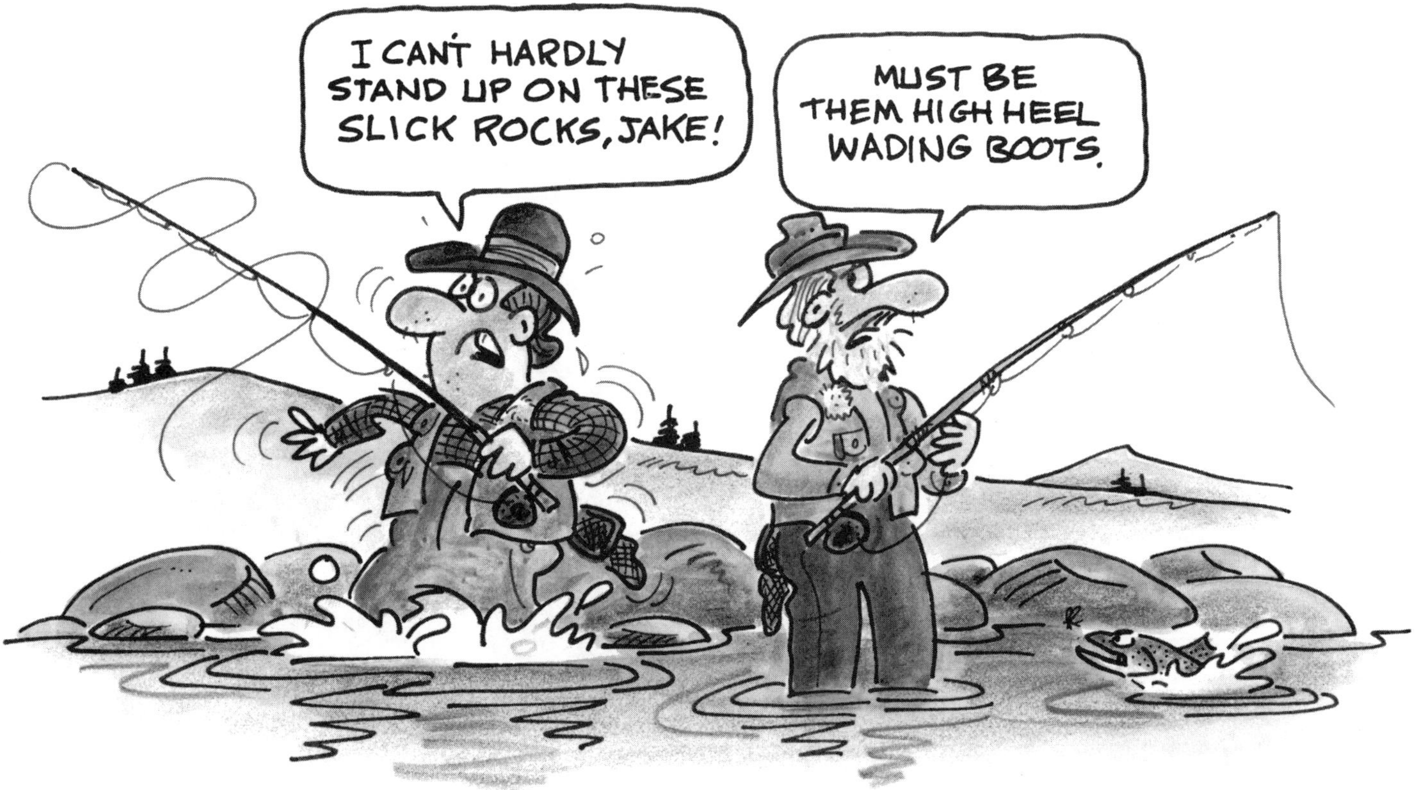

I CAN'T HARDLY STAND UP ON THESE SLICK ROCKS, JAKE!
MUST BE THEM HIGH HEEL WADING BOOTS.

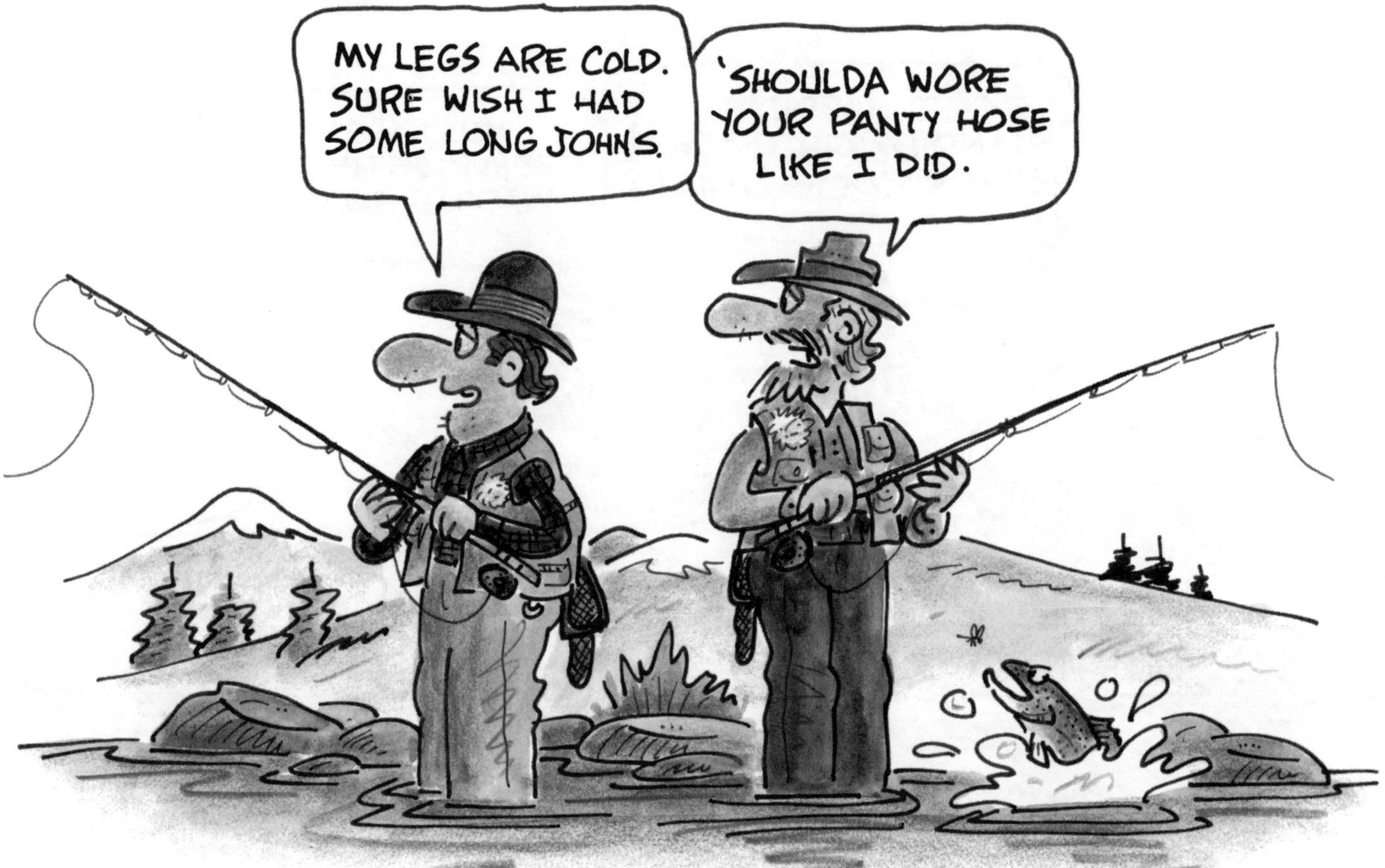
MY LEGS ARE COLD. SURE WISH I HAD SOME LONG JOHNS.
'SHOULDA WORE YOUR PANTY HOSE LIKE I DID.

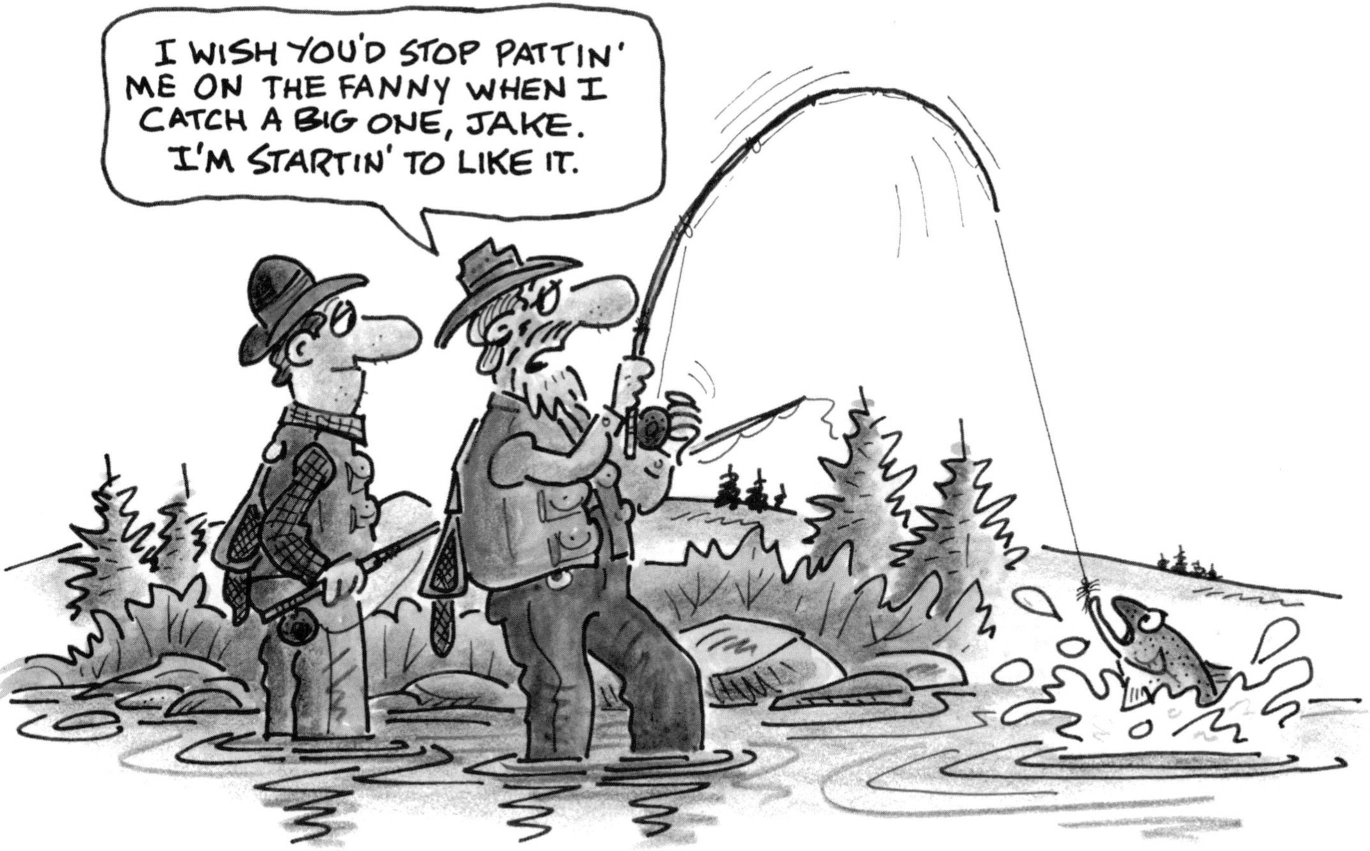
I WISH YOU'D STOP PATTIN' ME ON THE FANNY WHEN I CATCH A BIG ONE, JAKE. I'M STARTIN' TO LIKE IT.

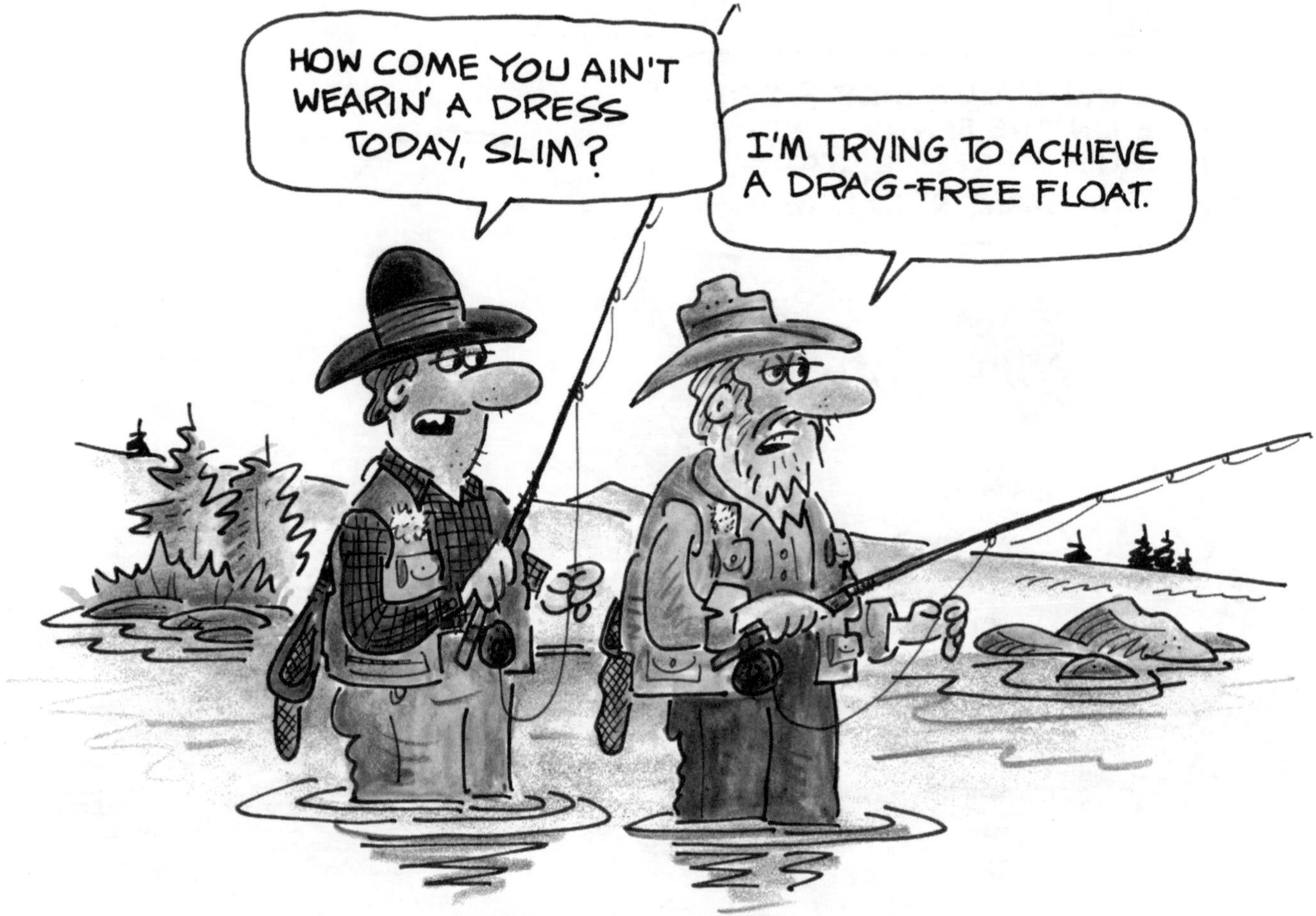
HOW COME YOU AIN'T WEARIN' A DRESS TODAY, SLIM?
I'M TRYING TO ACHIEVE A DRAG-FREE FLOAT.

NEW RULES

FOR TROUT FISHING

RULE #1

No more pink shirts or hats. And yes, they're PINK! Not coral or salmon. If you want us to take you seriously, stop buying your fishing clothes at Victoria's Secret.

RULE #2

Cell phones should be used on the stream only in cases of emergency, such as confirming a dinner date with Ashley Judd. We don't need to hear you begging your brother-in-law to loan you twenty bucks till payday.

RULE #3

Unless you are under sixteen years of age or it's your very first trout, don't ask someone to take your picture holding up a thirteen inch rainbow. It's embarrassing.

RULE #4

Leave your Rottweiler and your pit bull at home. You'll be talking to my attorney if old Fang decides to use my leg for a chewy toy.

RULE #5

Listen up, Tarzan. No matter how hot it is, put a shirt on under that vest. OK? We're tired of looking at your hairy, sunburned shoulders and bulging beer gut.

RULE #6

Stop asking the kid behind the counter in the big box store what they're hitting on. He was working in men's underwear yesterday, he'll be working in children's toys tomorrow, and he knows less about fishing than you do.

RULE #7

Ladies, don't be offended if we drop the old waders and answer the call of nature in your presence. When you tuck that ponytail up under your cap and get all wrapped up in a fleece pull-over, vest, and chest waders, we probably don't even realize you're female.

RULE #9

No more river dropping. You may have fished the Big Horn yesterday and the Yellowstone and the Madison the day before. Just don't tell everyone in the fly shop about it. We don't care.

...BLAH BLAH BIG HORN... BLAH BLAH SAN JUAN... BLAH BLAH BLAH...

RULE #8

Stop yelling at your buddy 300 yards downstream every time you get a strike. Did he ask you to report in every time your strike indicator disappeared? The rest of us don't care, and your buddy probably doesn't either. Act like you've caught a trout before.

RULE #10

Attention, fly shop owners! Stop telling us "the only way to fool these trout is with #28 emergers and 7X tippets." A trout's brain is the size of a soy bean and before he got out of the hatchery two days ago, he was scarfing down Purina Trout Kibbles and loving them.

MOST GUIDES ARE CONSCIENTIOUS, HARD WORKING INDIVIDUALS WHO SERVE THEIR CLIENTS WELL. BUT UNFORTUNATELY, ONCE IN A WHILE, YOU MAY FIND YOURSELF PAIRED UP WITH ...

THE **GUIDE** FROM **HELL!**

HARRY HANGOVER

Harry shows up late and hung over. When the hot sun hits the river you can smell the alcohol sweat seeping out of his pores. He wants to quit at mid-afternoon even though you've paid for a full day on the water. Finally, when he barfs over the gunwale, you agree to call it a day. Then he gets mad when you won't tip him.

MR. ENTHUSIASM

Conceived in a drift boat, born in a fly shop, Mr. Enthusiasm loves to fish. In fact he loves it so much he spends the day fishing instead of helping YOU. He makes as many casts as you do, putting his fly into the most likely spots before you have a chance at them. He catches a lunker and gets YOU to take HIS picture. By late afternoon, you're rowing the boat while Mr. Enthusiasm fishes.

THE ENTERTAINER

The entertainer doesn't realize his job is to put you where the trout are and help you catch them if necessary. He thinks it's his duty to entertain you all day. He spends the day boring you with stories and jokes, most of which you heard in high school. You half expect him to break out a banjo or start tap dancing.

THE BEGGAR

It's obvious from the outset that The Beggar is bucking for a big tip by playing on your sympathy. He talks constantly about his expenses and his family problems. He tells you his wife left him, and you can understand why. He says he needs $5000 by noon or his boat will be repossessed. You miss several strikes because of the tears in your eyes.

THE COMMENTATOR

You went fishing to get away from the world for a while, but you won't have that opportunity when you fish with The Commentator. He talks constantly about politics, religion, and other serious topics. By late afternoon you feel like you've spent the day in a boat with James Carville.

ANDY AMATEUR

It doesn't take long to figure out that Andy doesn't know any more about fishing this river than you do, and possibly less. He doesn't know a blood knot from a perfection loop, and he keeps asking YOU what fly to use. You finally spot a pod of rising trout and Andy runs the drift boat over them. You are probably Andy's first client... and possibly his last.

COOL NEW TROUT FISHING STUFF YOU CAN'T LIVE WITHOUT

Following the current trend to its logical conclusion, the new **MINUS 30 WEIGHT FLY ROD** is so light it has no action at all. Ideal for extremely small creeks and weak, sickly little fish.

You'll have that crowded western stream all to yourself when you activate your new **GRIZZLY GROWLER** audio tape. Just punch play and watch your fellow anglers scramble for safety.

Discourage rowdies in rubber rafts from violating your personal stream space by sinking a few of them with your combination **WADING STAFF AND BLOW GUN.**

Can't get everything you need for a day on the stream in your vest?
You need the new **TROUT TRAILER.** This warehouse on
pontoons holds the inventory of an entire fly shop.

Tired of searching through all those little vest pockets for your woollybuggers, your split shot, or your tippet material? Say goodbye to that problem with your new **ONE HUGE POCKET VEST.** Available in coral, sunglow, and British tan.

FIREHOLE MADISON

ANSWERS YOUR TROUT FISHING QUESTIONS!

Noted guide, innovative fly tyer, and long time editor of *LIP RIPPER* magazine, this pundit of the pools has helped several generations of fishermen solve their angling problems. Here now are some of the most frequently asked questions Madison has fielded over the years, along with his insightful answers.

Q: Are you familiar with an olive woollybugger?

A: Are you kidding? I dated her in high school.

Q: What's your favorite rock tune?

A: "Can't Get No Caddis Action" by The Rolling Stone Flies.

Q: Do you pay any attention to the solunar tables?

A: No. My wife picks out the furniture at our house.

Q: Have you ever caught Dolly Varden?

A: Not in person, but I've seen her on TV.

Q: Have you ever spent an evening digging night crawlers?

A: I don't dig ANY of those heavy metal groups.

Q: How do you catch small mouth?

A: From a public drinking fountain or by kissing someone who has it.

Q: Do you practice catch and release?

A: Only with women.

Q: What's the best line you've ever used?

A: I think it was, "If I could rearrange the alphabet I'd put U and I together, Baby."

Q: Can you tie a blood knot?

A: Are you kidding? I don't even own a tie.

Q: Many anglers use polarized glasses. Do you recommend them?

A: Nope. I drink right out of the bottle.

Q: I took my son trout fishing but when I showed him how to clean a fish he threw up. How should I handle this situation?

A: Your son is a sissy. Forget about taking him fishing and enroll him in ballet lessons.

Q: In cold weather, do you wear long johns under your waders?

A: Hey, do I ask *you* about *your* underwear.

Q: What could be more exciting than hooking up with a ten pound rainbow on a gravel bar?

A: Hooking up with a 140 pound bimbo in a singles bar.

Q: Have you ever gone out and caught something after dark?

A: No, I've been lucky so far.

Q: Have you ever used a Parmachene Belle?

A: No, but I've BEEN used by a SOUTHERN belle.

Q: Do you ever fish with ants?

A: No, but I've fished with my Uncle Marvin and my brother-in-law.

Q: What do you think of salmon eggs?

A: They're not just for breakfast anymore.

Q: You've been quoted as saying that nothing could put a bend in your rod like a ten pound brown. Do you still feel that way?

A: That was before I met Darlene in Kansas City.

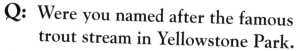

Q: Were you named after the famous trout stream in Yellowstone Park.

A: No. I was named after a painful medical condition.

Q: Do you think it's fair to catch the Browns when they're spawning?

A: Hey, I never spy on my neighbors and I hope they don't spy on me.

Q: I've heard that Native Americans made protective gear by stretching brook trout skins over a willow framework. What were these devices called?

A: Brook Shields.

Q: As a fly tyer, what's your favorite vise?

A: It's a toss-up between shooting craps and fishing with dynamite.

Q: What do you think of the Copper John?

A: It's very uncomfortable on a cold night.

Q: What's the Latin name for a blue winged olive?

A: El Buggo.

AFTER A HARD DAY ON THE STREAM IT'S NICE TO RELAX WITH A **SERIOUS CARD GAME**

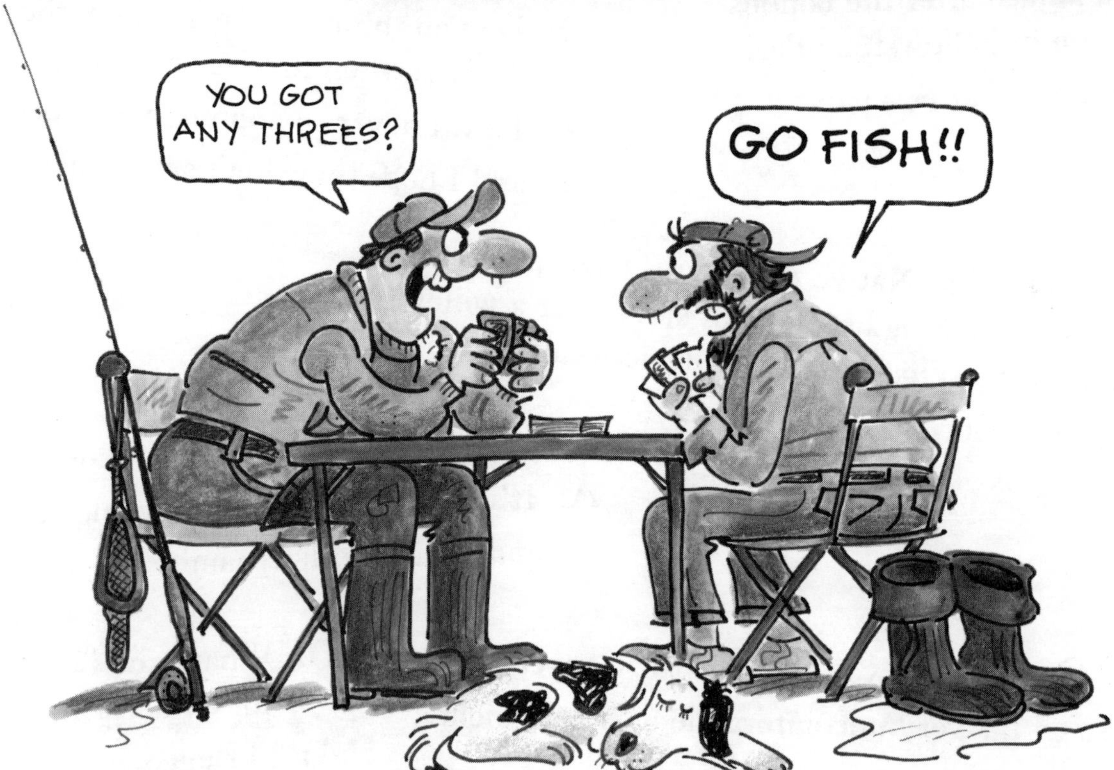
YOU GOT ANY THREES?
GO FISH!!

TV NEWS FOR THE TROUT FISHERMAN.

F ORGET HOUSE FIRES, CAR WRECKS, AND MURDERS... TELL US THE **IMPORTANT STUFF!**

JOE SMITH CAUGHT A 5 LB. BROWN BELOW THE HIGHWAY BRIDGE ON A BLACK WOOLLY-BUGGER... RAINBOWS ARE HITTING SCUDS ON THE EAST FORK... SHADY CREEK IS MUDDY BUT CLEARING...

TAKE YOUR DOG
Trout Fishing

He will enjoy getting acquainted
with other anglers on the stream…

And your fellow fishermen will enjoy meeting him as well.

When other anglers bring their dogs, your dog will make friends with his canine brothers and sisters.

If you're lucky enough to hook that fish of a lifetime,
your dog will even provide invaluable help in landing it...

And on those slow days when there's no action,
you will enjoy your dog's companionship.

THIS HAPPENED TO ME!

Incredible adventures of actual anglers just like YOU in the watery world of trout.

I attempted to wade across a popular tailwater during a discharge. The water was higher and deeper than I had anticipated and I was swept off my feet and drowned. I'm now in heaven, which is okay, I guess. But I had always hoped to go to Montana.

While I was napping on the bank of a well known stream, a beaver ate my bamboo fly rod that has been in my family for four generations. The next day I picked through seven piles of scat, hoping the beaver had passed the rod, but all I ever found was the reel seat and three guides.

After a fishless day on the river with an incompetent guide I tried to get away without tipping him. Being a rather large fellow, he grabbed me by my ankles, turned me upside down, and shook me 'til my wallet fell out, then helped himself to its entire contents.

While relieving myself on the stream bank
I saw a large trout rise to a floating mayfly.
I quickly grabbed my rod and cast to the
behemoth before pulling my waders up,
hooking myself in a very painful area,
and spending the rest of the day in the ER.

I was eating my streamside lunch when a very large trout leapt from the water and tried to devour my peanut butter sandwich. Fortunately it stuck to the roof of his mouth and I was able to retrieve it with only minor damage to my hand.

While fishing a small stream that runs under the runway of our local airport I hooked an incoming 747 on my back cast. For a split second it gave me quite a tussle. Had I landed it, it would have been a world record for 4X tippet.

When noon came on an all day float trip my guide discovered that he had forgotten to pack our lunch. Luckily he always brings along some salmon eggs and night crawlers for clients who can't get the hang of fly fishing. We managed to subsist on these until dinnertime, but a good chardonnay would have been a welcome addition to our meal.

While wading a scenic mountain stream I came upon a redneck and his mate washing his pickup truck in a low water crossing. When I whipped out my cell phone and called the local sheriff to complain about the environmental degradation they were causing, the sheriff turned out to be the redneck's brother-in-law. My court date is next Tuesday.

THE FUTURE OF TROUT FISHING

In order to fish our most popular streams you will need to call ahead and make a reservation.

Once you have your reservation and have reported to the river warden at the designated time and date, you will be given a number and directed to the waiting area assigned to anglers from your zip code.

When your number is called you will be directed to the Risk Management office where it will be determined if you meet the necessary physical requirements to fish your assigned area.

If you qualify, you will be instructed to sign a waiver releasing
the State Fish and Game Department from all liability.

You will then be escorted to your assigned rock in the river and given your fishing instructions.

Remember, you are here to have fun. Please fish as rapidly as possible in order to make the most of your allotted hour on the river.

A GALLERY OF CARTOONS FOR THE TROUT FISHERMAN

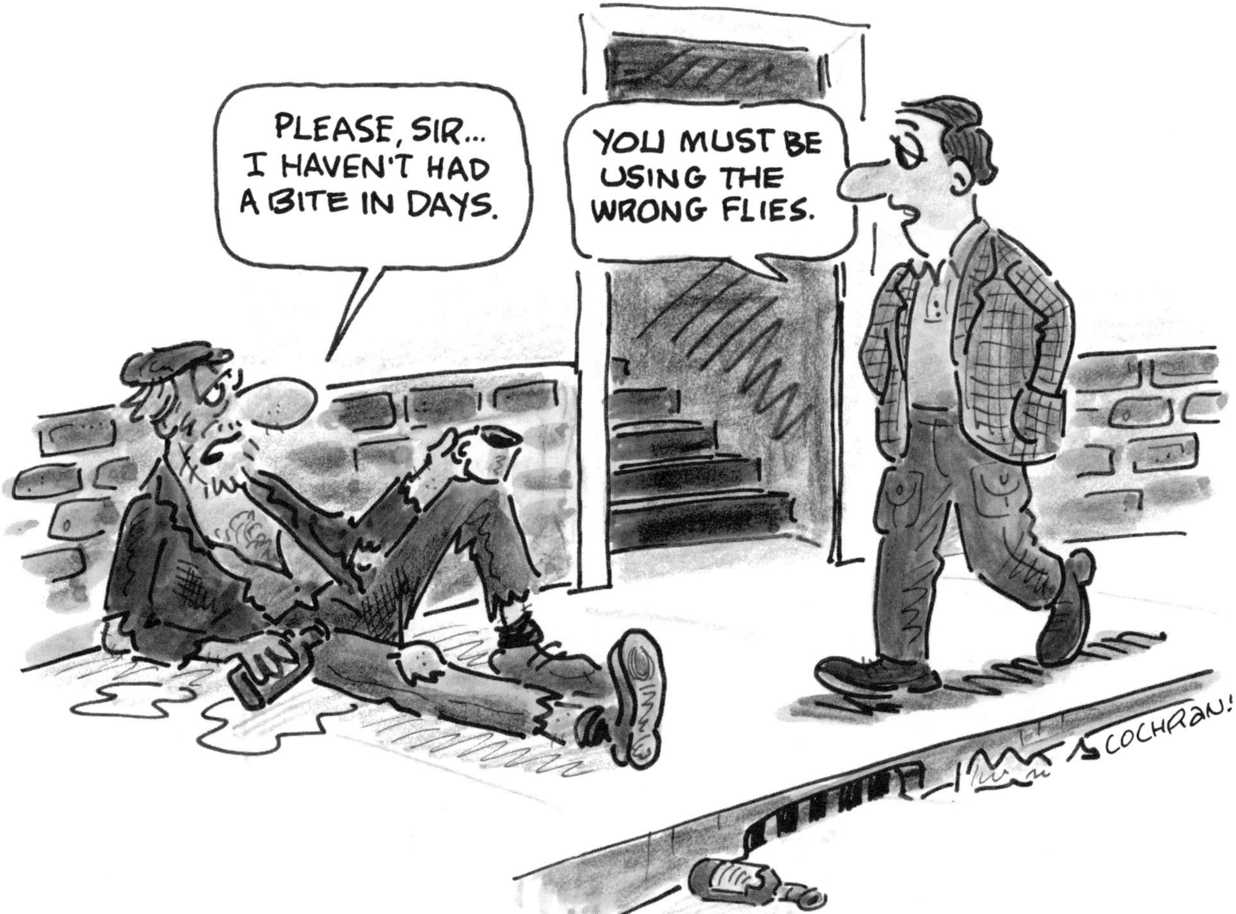
PLEASE, SIR...
I HAVEN'T HAD
A BITE IN DAYS.
YOU MUST BE
USING THE
WRONG FLIES.
COCHRAN!

"I think I just put some cargo in these cargo pants!"

"Today we're going to learn the double surgeon's knot."

"I take it you're not totally committed to catch-and-release."

"Look, Darlene! A 200 pounder! Let's catch him
and take his picture, then turn him loose."

WALLY WOOLLYBUGGER GOES TO A SHRINK

"I want a fly that speaks out to the very soul of the trout! A charismatic fly, delicate yet durable! A fly that can successfully compete with naturals on the water and fairly SCREAMS out in no uncertain terms… BITE ME!!"

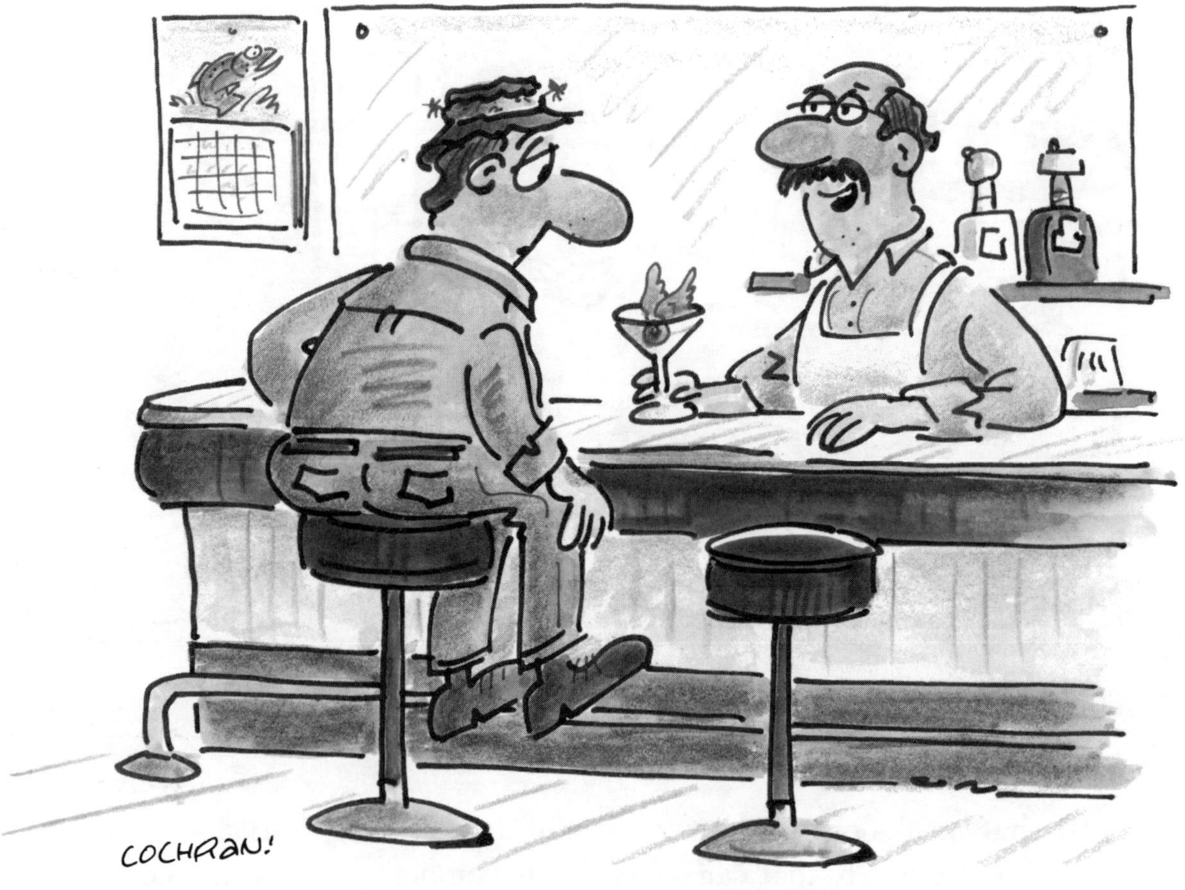
COCHRAN!

"It's a blue winged olive."

"When they release you, float downstream belly-up
for a few yards. It scares the hell out of them."

"You may be interested in joining our caught-and-released support group."

"Out of the way, sub-human bait-dunking redneck scum! A FLY FISHERMAN is coming!"

"With all due respect, Your Honor, I don't believe
you're giving this case the attention it deserves.

"You never knew your cousin Marvin. He was sold to a salmon egg company and used for bait.

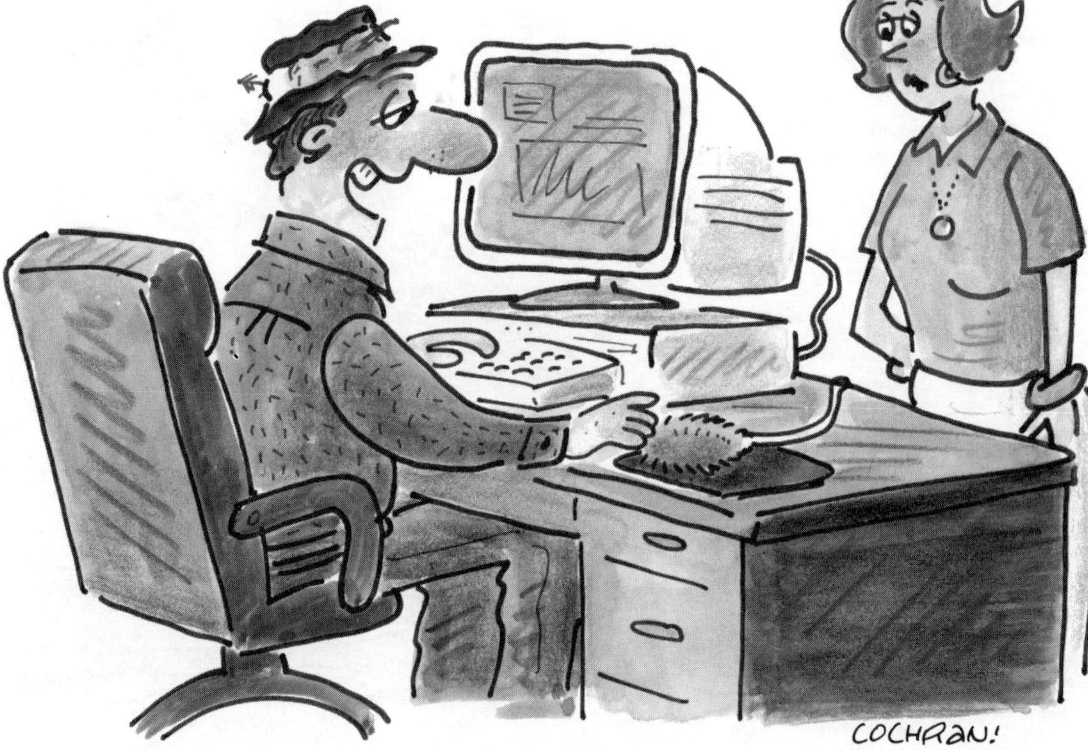
COCHRAN!

“It’s a deer hair mouse.”

"Perrier bottles… caviar boxes… I wish yuppies had never taken up trout fishing."

The End